Maurice Henry Hewlett

Songs and Meditations

Maurice Henry Hewlett

Songs and Meditations

ISBN/EAN: 9783741187001

Manufactured in Europe, USA, Canada, Australia, Japa

Cover: Foto ©Angelika Wolter / pixelio.de

Manufactured and distributed by brebook publishing software
(www.brebook.com)

Maurice Henry Hewlett

Songs and Meditations

SONGS AND MEDITATIONS

BY

MAURICE HEWLETT

'Di rime sparse il suono'

WESTMINSTER

ARCHIBALD CONSTABLE

AND CO. 1896

PREFATORY NOTE

Of the poems in this book, those printed
on pages 32, 65, 116, have appeared in the
Academy, that on page 21 in the *Pall Mall
Gazette*. I am indebted to the Editors of
these journals for permission to reprint
them here. None of the others have been
published, so far as I remember.

London, *October* 1896.

CONTENTS

SONGS

b   ix

CONTENTS

MEDITATIONS

CONTENTS

SONGS

A

A HYMN TO ARTEMIS

Queen of the upper air, crown'd Artemis!
Quick-girdled huntress and moon-diadem'd,
O patroness of all our keen endeavour,
Lady that life from life dost sever,
Hear thou from haunt Eubœan!
Life out of life, seed unto seed thou givest,
Thou potent in the Stygian shades infernal
As in the blue supernal;
Potent thou too in the green habitations
Of teeming Earth, whose nations
Adore in thee their holiest aspirations,

3

See their wholesome, see their pure
Stroke and striving imaged sure
In thine implacable, chaste, thy virgin medi-
    tations.

Thee crocus-vested Caryatides
Intone with long-drawn pæan;
To thee the parsley crown, the pure libation,
The youngling hind, we offer up, so soon
Within her sapphire cave the moon
Swingeth her frosted lamp, and silver stars
    their station
About her take, and beacon over seas:
To thee come languid mothers, children at
    their knees,
Thee virgins not yet wedded
Seek first and offer up the tress new-shredded,
And snowy maiden smock;

A HYMN TO ARTEMIS

To thee, as to a rock
Of succour in wild seas, the girdle ivory-headed
That guards the blossom of breasts by men
    unheeded.

When Delos, driven out by stress of weather,
Had roam'd the vasty sea a restless course
Vexèd, so soon that Leto's aching feet
Were cooled, her nine days' anguish ended;
In that great peace that followed
Came order out of chaos, the Sun threw out,
And in the windless caverns of night
Sail'd serene the silver Moon.
Thereon, because a calm miraculous
Follow'd the great twin birth of light and
    light,
God said, ' Delos the chosen is and shall be;
Star-ray for all this blind and groping Earth.'

5

SONGS

Dreadful thou art and sudden !

Madness is thine and horror unavailing,

The woe of women wailing

(Niobe wailing for her sons and daughters),

And shriek of starven madness :

Anon the swiftsure of death, the closing of
  waters—

Dark, slippery, swift, pathless, untrod—

'Reeling over our heads, swaying our hair

Suckt like weed : bubbles of air

Mark for a moment the place where the
  wretch of despair

Sank at thy stare.

Thou to be sought in dewy Arcadian haunts,

Soothest, chastest and cleanest !

Where broodeth the dove, where the wood
  pecker chants

A HYMN TO ARTEMIS

His mocking refrain.
Sacred to thee are birds of the air, and all cattle,
The mountain track, the glade where in battle,
Clashing their antler'd heads, stags beat amain
Earth for the herd's dominion :
Thee glorify the hawks, each strain of the pinion
Is as a hymn of thy praise, swifter than sight !
For in thee the gladness of strength, and beauty
of strength,
In thee the clearness of light and throbbing of
light,
Have all their crown, O deathless Queen of the
night,
Amarynthinian !

All that is gracious and suave in a maid,
All fearless and flawless in chastely carved lips,
All that is proud in her eyes, intent, unafraid,

What there may be in the touch of her finger-
    tips;

The reticence of her and modesty, keeping apart,

The joyance of swift light motion, throat to the
    day;

All the glowing abandon that beats in her heart,

All the love she knoweth but shunneth to say:

The rapture of living, love's growing, the babe

That seeketh the breast—

They are thine, Lady, that figurest all, having
    all

That is pure at thy hest!

ODE TO THE DAWN OF ITALY

(PARABASIS FROM A PLAY)

As to a mountain holy
Peakt in a haze of live blue trembling air,
Anointed by the glory of the Sun,
So faltering as a pilgrim, faint and slowly
I lift up wearied eyes
To this vague land that lies
As a tired queen ere her long day begun,
Breasting the Southern glamour, and slaves
    the North
To fan the tresses of her heavy hair,
And with her stretchèd palms draws East
    and West in one.

9

SONGS

O still I hail thee, since most fair art thou,
Lady of smooth broad brow
And healing touch !
Thou that abidest where the Adrian brims,
And where spreads reedy silver Thrasymene
One sheeted broad demesne ;
Or in dark Tyrrhene seas where daylight dims,
And men, fainting through much
Toil, seek with their blind hands
To bind about their brows thy hair in thick wet
    bands.

For rest is in thine eyes,
And full of rest thy voice
Calling among the water-brooks of easeful things;
Sweet-cool the winnowings,
And full of solace when the sun-glare dies
The play of thy great wings

ODE TO THE DAWN OF ITALY

Across the thick of evening dusk with
    hidden noise.
So on the breast of Night,
Beneath thy serious eyes,
Wrapt in the silver light
About thy head that lies,
Lull'd by the mysteries
And soft low breathings of thy deep delight,
Let me faint out of strife where Sleep is
    Death's surmise.

Awake, O thou most holy,
O Bride desirable of all the Earth !
Lift up thy languid head, the languid lids
Droopt on thy solemn eyes, the moment bids
We front the world with mirth.
Awake the tired, the lowly
Raise thou !   Lo, priest-like Dawn

SONGS

Stoled all in swathes of lawn
And shrouded gossamer: lo! he will
    hymn the morn.

I sing thine eager rising
With music on thy lips,
With fresh dew in thy hair
And on the rosy tips
Of thy quick fingers prayer
Like balm to anoint our faint souls
    agonising :
I see the Bridegroom issue,
I see the dead wake up
And all wan faces quiver,
As in a rain-fed river
The stream out-brims the cup;
Then, veil'd in golden tissue,
Phœbus the chant take up !

ODE TO THE DAWN OF ITALY

Surely now, surely succour cometh in,
Surely is paid the sin,
And past the burthen of night!
For here in cooler air
The autumn day smiles meekly, a kinder death
Than threaten'd us beneath
The restless crave and hunger of the sea!

Behold! our lord the Sun,
Apollo's panoplied arm,
Streameth out of the gates
And fireth the ways of dawn,
And kindleth the scars of the hill-tops one after
    one
With the flush of Heaven's quick fire:
Even so is my own desire
Litten, and hope leapeth higher and higher:
Lift up your voice to the Queen in her bride's
    attire!

13

THE CRETAN ODE

(PARADASIS FROM A PLAY)

FIRST I salute you, guardian hills of Crete,
With careful brows and hands uplifted high—
Dicté, where in cold splendours of the moon
The lonely Goddess dwells, from whose bare crag
Maid Britomartis, virgin shy and pure,
Cast all her delicate treasure to the sea
And by death saved her life ; next, Ida, thee,
Veil'd in thine immemorial cypress robes,
Dark with the murmurs of perpetual peace,
Ida, whose haunts Zeus knew, and loveth still.
And also you, O holiest sentinels
About Cydonia ramparting the sea !

14

THE CRETAN ODE

Sisters, who linkt in ice
With glittering crowns a-row,
Watch over Crete while night pursueth day,
And fiercer than day's light
Dazzle all eyes that dare affront your beams.
O ye dread haunts of God, by man untrodden,
Only by man adored from very far!
By that great strength ye are,
Holding a steadfast way
Through good and ill report,
Through tempest and dismay,
Through blinding snow and frost;
Ye only that abide
Where all is chance and change, for no man liveth
Who knew or heard his fathers tell that day
When ye were not inflexible as now!—
Listen, each haunted place,
Ye hills, each crown'd with God,

SONGS

Listen, most evil case
Is on us, our feet have trod
The splintry steep that leadeth men astray ,
By pain from Heaven's clear way :
We have slipt in our own blood,
And each new morn hath summon'd wearier day.

Wherefore, seeing to no man it is given
To read the will of Heaven ;
Seeing the blessèd Gods remotely reign,
Not pitying our pain,
Nor stooping down at all, rather pursuing
Their sport in our undoing ;
It doth become that man whose love is law
To clothe himself with awe,
And gazing on your strength win strength to
    abide
What fortune may betide.

THE CRETAN ODE

Yet, O ye patron Gods, who watch our going,
Withal unfathomable and unseen,
Withal aloof and ruthless, no man liveth
To dare against ye any rite undone;
Nor can remove his eyes
From your reflected state,
Knowing how excellently great
Ye are, how beauteous, swift, supremely wise,
Nor stay to seek (since without beauty dies
Man's better part) uncheckt that thing he
    flies!
Therefore to you, swift pair,
Whom patient Leto bore your Father Zeus
In Delos mid the folded Cyclades,
To thee, O Archer-Phœbus, to whom the
    Sun
Is but a mantle flaming at the edge;
Thee, Hymnia, stripling huntress of the air,

SONGS

To whom soothsay pertains
And keener shafts than ever arrow shot—
Lo now, in perilous pass I bring you my despair.

Eileithyia, thee next I invoke,
As women when the stroke
Of their most heavy pains
Falleth, and new life strains,
And their fray'd life to meet it maketh stress,
Yet often fainteth out through feebleness !
O who with bent down head
Dost hang above the bed,
And with thy torch's light
Direct the new-born sight
Unto thy holy face,
That its first view be grace !
Be merciful ere all our land
Faileth, bid stay the hand

THE CRETAN ODE

Red to the wrist with carnage, that it cease
And the end be peace !

And thou, demesned in Crete,
O Queen Demeter, watchful over wheat !
And lonely Mother long inured to pain ;
If now a little thought of our fair fields
Linger in thee who blest them once,
What time by Ida's valleys thou wert glad
When the green corn peer'd out
Glimmering upon the brown and dusty
    earth :—
So do thou turn thine eyes,
If not remote in grief,
If not preoccupied
By thine absorbing ever-pressing lack,
Lest all indeed should die as some have
    died !

SONGS

Haply the Gods may hear, for Crete is shrill,
Being wounded ; they may pity, for Crete is fair
For all her peakt complaining, as a maid
Stolen for some lord's pleasure waxeth frail,
And in her frailty more desirable.
But an they choose not, I as one grown old,
Hardened to storm and cold,
Will set my face as yours to fires and chills,
O immemorial Hills !

WAR-SONGS FOR THE ENGLISH

I. SENNET

ENGLAND, my country, my pride,
Mother and Queen, I the weak
In all else but my praise,
To thee, Mother, I speak.
If the World, hungry-eyed,
Carp at thy glory, or raise
Outcry, or, tongue in the cheek,
Scoff thee, seek to deride
Thine onset too great and too wide
For envy to hinder or check—
Think, O Mother, thy bays
Our blood hath water'd, thy side
Is girt with our sword ; our days
Are thy days : be not denied.

SONGS

While England stands in the sea
The sea is hers; where the wind
Bloweth from England, her grace
Spreadeth her seignory.
From pole to pole is her fee,
She knoweth not strength to bind,
To slow or stay her; her face
Setteth out: but behind
The grieving horde snappeth free
And snarleth a sour grimace,
And thinketh our England blind
When she letteth them be,
And holdeth her ancient place.

But an the outcry swelleth
Too angry or vext in her ear,
Or one perchance of the rout
Poketh his searching snout

WAR-SONGS FOR THE ENGLISH

To coign of earth wherein dwelleth
One of her cubs; should she hear
The clash of arms, or the shout
Of battle ring; if she smelleth
The blood and smoke—without fear,
Without haste, with most sober cheer
She maketh ready: no flout
Stayeth her to come out
There where the trumpet foretelleth
Battle of peer with peer.

When she loost from her lair,
The grey she-lion, she stood
Proud and shaking, and lo!
Her lips curl'd back, her teeth bare,
Hinted the surge of her mood.
In her fierce eyes the blank glare
Of a light recess'd and aglow

Dared her to be withstood.
So in old days of her blood,
So when her pride in flood
Leapt, she remember'd her blow
Of Grenville and Churchill and Hood.
So she remembers now.

And England struck, and her stroke
Was heavy, and all men's breath
Stay'd to see her, and hail'd
England armour'd in oak.
Oak without, but beneath
Surged and pulsed, facing Death,
The heart that never yet fail'd,
The red that never yet paled,
The tongue that never shame spoke.
Sons ! now heed her, she saith
' O Sons, I am slow to provoke,

Slow to wrath; I have quail'd
Only to sin.   Now my teeth
Are set.   What is mine, be it held.'

Seed of England, O seed
Of the pack that hunted Poictiers,
Your fathers saw Nelson bleed
In Victory's hour, on her deck;
And their fathers heard with glad ears
The song of the Wolfe of Quebec!
Shall ye now, in the need
Of our Mother, hold you in check?
Shall ye sit and babble of fears?
Ye will not!   The sword is freed,
The flag floateth, and quick
Shrilleth the cry—' Ho! take heed:
Heed what ye speak : England hears.'

SONGS

II. RALLY

To ye, whose tongue is our Shakespeare's, I
    speak :
   England hath need of her men—
Sons of the ancient East, ye of the ardent West,
    Ye of the sword, of the pen ;
All who confess England Mother, who suckt
    At her mighty breast,
Who drank of her milk, who bear on their brows
    the mark
    Of her vigilant crest.
Rise now, Australia, Canada ! rise
    India, Africa !
Speakers of English speech, servants of English
    Gods,
    Rise, it is war ! it is war !

England has never bow'd, England is quiet and
    proud,
    Her children are free
In all save this, to rally to England's nod
    For her dignity.
Brothers, the fates are fixt, nothing can stay
    England's decree :—
'This much is mine to possess it; I must be
    queen
    Over land and sea.'
Choose, choose, O English, follow the Fates
    Whither they lead,
Or sink back to the ruck, to the trough of the
    coward :
    Choose ye with speed !
And to ye, once rebel, still kindred, our England
    speaks,
    ' By your ancient fires,

O by the common cradle, the larger blood
  Of our common sires !
The foe shrieketh, the German, the Frenchman,
   the Slav,
  Grown covetous,
Murmur, mutter, bluster—England alone !
  Who is for us ? '
Nay, who is not for England, speaking her
   speech,
  Sharing her fame ?
Will brother deliver brother to alien death,
  Or wink on his shame ?
O ye brothers of us, ye separate sons
  Of England our Mother,
Sons of Alfred and Edward, of Richard the Lion,
  Of Harry, what other
Road will ye tread ? the road that even is red
  With the harvest of spears,

Or the road of the base, cluster'd with Panic and
    Sloth
    And their huddle of fears ?
Choose, choose, America, England awaits
    Her eldest-born's choice :
Choose, lose no time, already the rest of us
    shout
    With one single voice—
    England, Mother, rejoice !
For England, hemm'd by her resolute sons,
    setteth out,
    And neither her foes' nor thy choice
Will hinder her path or turn her purpose about !

SONGS

III. CLARION

Who that hath ever heard
  His Mother's song hath not leapt,
Or her crying and hath not stirr'd?

  Who in her need hath slept,
In her plenty hath not rejoiced,
  At thought of her shame not wept?

Voice above all we have voiced
  Is hers of the clarion shrill
And hers of the flag we hoist :—

  England, our Mother still,
Our haven girdling in sea
  Woodland and grassy hill;

30

WAR-SONGS FOR THE ENGLISH

England, born to be free
  As the wind that drives in her face
Or the wave on weather and lee!

  Let her but hint disgrace
On one bearing her name,
  Her sons take their silent place

Rankt to do out the blame,
  To wash the escutcheon clean,
To spend blood for her fame.

  O English, the war-breath is keen
Now: ye have understood
  Our mother's menace, I ween.

  Being of the English blood,
  Are ye to be withstood?
  Are ye in whimpering mood?
  No, by the living God!

DIVÆ GENETRICIS LAUDES

THE streaming skies have wept our lonely death;
  Straighten'd we lie and hapless wait for thee:
Thou art our Mother! warm us with thy breath;

  Whether within a hollow of the sea,
Or in some yet unravisht dell of cresses,
  Or ferny thicket where no frost may be,

Thou dwellest, or where desolate cypresses
  Toss their black plumes about in thin blue air,
And wailing seas fling high their stormy tresses;

  Lo, in thy myrtle groves the doves prepare
Their homesteads, and their broodful murmurs
      float
Out to the wintry beam, and here and there

DIVÆ GENETRICIS LAUDES

The ousel thrills his mellow-chorded rote,
  And in broad diapason all thy choir
Prelude the rapture of thy honey throat.

  Now in the drenchèd pasture spire on spire
Uplifts the tender undergrowth of grasses ;
  Now the sun tinges blushing woods with fire

Where, westering tardier, glowing he passes,
  As loath to miss thy coming when from over
The even sea thou glidest ; white-arm'd lasses

  Lapful of meadow flowers stray to discover
The crocus' purple chalice gemm'd with gold,
  And pencill'd wood-sorrel, shy April's lover,

To deck thy sylvan altar.   Now, behold !
  The sacrifice, fruit from thine Earth's warm
      breast,
Balm and new milk, the firstlings of the fold,

SONGS

Rose-sharded wind-flowers, and garlands drest
For festival, and glossy eggs of doves
   Fresh taken from the sanctuary nest.

So, Aphroditè, grey-eyed queen of loves,
   So, Earth-begetter, full of tilth and store,
   Rise from the dead, nor leave us any more,
Fountain and stream of everything that moves !

DAUGHTER OF EARTH

I WILL make an altar of earth
With myrtle deckt and with yew,
Covered with sods: the dew
Shall wash it dainty and clean.
I raise it, O Child, to you;
To the peace you have, and the mirth,
To the wells of love in your eyes
And the sweet tide of your breath,
To your young blood ere it dries;
To Innocence, Ardour, and You.

Hymnia you shall be call'd;
For worship of you the shrine
Is built of pure thought, and fine

SONGS

As the mould of your shapeliness.
Let Summer breathe on it, and bees,
And the wind's love ; from the vine
I borrow clinging ; let Dawn
Greet you thro' lattice of trees—
Plane, and Poplar that sighs,
And Lime, the lover of bees.

Smooth, rounded, and knit
As the fashion of perfect limbs
I would have it be : of your eyes
I ask for the sanctities
Of their violet glint ere it dims
To kindle the fire on it.
Above the green altar-ledge
Still, incessant, your eyes
Fire the dusk : they are lit
From the love in my heart that lies.

DAUGHTER OF EARTH

Give of your hair to hide
The altar-house ; spray it wide
In a silk mesh—ah, my pride !
Was ever iconostase
So superbly bedeckt
With warm brown curtain, or fleckt
As this with rays of the sun ?
Or when since Mass was begun
Came priest to cover his face
In so burnisht curtain and wide ?

Your breath is for incense-flight
From the censer pure of your mouth :
It is odorous of the South
And the pastures of all the West.
The wet fresh growth of the year,
Honeysuckle and thyme,
Anemones meek as death,

SONGS

Crocuses yellow and white :
All shy blossoms are here
Nurst in your balmy breath.

For altar-stone is your lap
Whereon, a pure offering,
I lay down flowers, a song,
A bird's dropt feather, a ring
Woven of scented rush
For my spousal with Earth.   And I crush
From mallows the milky sap,
Flour from the burnt brown wheat,
And from limes the honey, to make
For the altar a fairy cake.

Kneeling I lift eyes up
The ripple of you, and see
As a bud stiff on her stalk
Your face in whose beam I walk

DAUGHTER OF EARTH

Lift from your gown's dark cup,
And your grave eyes fixt on me.
Then I fall, bending the knee,
For your mouth quivers, a tear
Veils your seeing : I know
Your heart's grief, O my dear !

Heaven kiss'd Earth and loved her
Face to face in the wild
Still deeps of a night
Once in June.   O Child,
Thou, pledge of delight,
Thou wert born of that night,
Spirit of Earth, the joy
Of whoso loveth cool rain,
And summer heats, and the pain
Of frosts, and spring's onset mild :—
Thou art Earth's quick-born child !

PROCESSIONAL

This is the holy day of half the year;
To Hymnia's pageant come, for it is here.

First, with shrill summons of the double reed
Let the flute-player bid the folk take heed.

Stand on one side, or follow in the throng
That like a dancing water laughs along,

Headed by maidens, tall and slim as wands,
With budded wreaths and sisterly linkt hands.

After them lads, clean in new snowy smocks,
Come, leading by the firstlings of their flocks;

PROCESSIONAL

And children let from school, in loose array,
Bare-legg'd, bare-arm'd, head-bare, busy with
    play.

Their wagging tongues make such a merry din
The piper's winding tune sounds far and thin.

Next girls, with viol tuckt against the cheek,
Trailing their long robes, bend like lilies meek ;

Even as the bow, drawn out by their lithe fingers,
Wounds slowly, so their passionate music lingers:

Till to a master-call awakes the morn,
And beasts leave graze to wonder at the horn.

The trumpeters in Lincoln green and tan,
Lusty as noon, make music while they can ;

SONGS

For homage is best done by man to maid
With plough and sheep-hook, reaping-hook and
  spade :

Only in May-time Rob, lagging with Prue,
Can belt her with his arm the whole day through,

And music only then her voice uprears
To honour him who sings and her who hears.

Now bend all knees, and off go every cap ;
Cast now, ye maids, the flowers from your lap !

Under a canopy of pink dog-rose
Young Hymnia a virgin-goddess goes.

In what sweet guise she cometh is well seen,
Close-robed in a thin garment, white and green ;

PROCESSIONAL

Long-throated, something tall, and sober-eyed,
With parted lips she takes the morning's pride.

And she is crown'd with wood-buds and young
   grass,
And balmy-breath'd as any country lass.

But for her gesture free and queenly mild
You had thought her a wood-girl, caged but wild.

No one is she of that brood unconfined,
A lonely presence without peer or kind.

But as the breathless glory when day breaks
Holds men, so all men's longing Hymnia takes.

So shy withal is she, and burning-pure,
Few find her, and few dare that only sure

Footway that leads through thicket, holt, and
    brake
To Hymnia's altar by the forest lake.

But they that toil, and carry in their hands
Clear offering, may see her where she stands

Recluse as violets, with dewy eyes
And bashful welcome and shy glad surprise,

At this, the time she best loves, when the
    earth
Quickens and throbs to put off winter dearth.

Through windy valleys now, like driven flame,
See her host flutter, calling her by name :—

' Hymnia, ah, Hymnia, thou pure Maid,
Come, for the earth is green, be not afraid ! '

PROCESSIONAL

Then she, demurely stoled in thoughtful youth,
Leadeth her homely pageant to the South ;

And after her this bridal company
Of youths and virgins suddenly let free,

Kissed on to frolic by the ardent wind,
Yet keeping innocence and honest mind.

For Hymnia's priest and priestess shall not fire
With any love but love of her desire ;

And her desire being all for wholesomeness,
Desire in them is rein'd by her duress.

Now go ye to your homes, the rites are done ;
And going, pray speed on the year begun.

CANZONE OF HYMNIA'S CORONATION

Bind for her head a crown of crocuses,
And since she is more fair
Than they 'twill win them honour
If they may cluster there,
Catching light from the glory of her hair,
As she goes coronall'd with crocuses
Set like a wreath upon her.

So soon the new-litten Sun
Beameth his golden eye upon the day,
And in the grass new breath doth stir,
O come, apparel her
In colours fresh as ever rainbow spun ;
Let us rejoice in her whenas we may.

CANZONE OF HYMNIA'S CORONATION

Bind for her head a crown of crocuses
Of white and mauve and yellow,
To kindle on her brows,
And grow demure and mellow
From being linkt to such a grave yokefellow :
Loveliness shines in maids and crocuses
The fairer for their snows.

And now smooth-vestured for delight
In a clear gown of blue and silver white,
She steppeth forth to the green
And pleasant fields ; unto her lovely face
The light doth look for food,
That thereon supping he may borrow grace
And for her sake live clean
To be a sweet shrine for such maidenhood.

Bind for her head a crown of crocuses
Or e'er the bride be married

SONGS

And stolen from her home :
Too long the bride hath tarried,
Across the threshold she must soon be carried.
Brides should be clothed like the March crocuses,
Soon made ready to come.

What bridal for what bride
Than Sun and open weather
Could be fitter her pride
Whom no man's yoke could tether ?
You shall but see together
Her and the South-west wind,
But you shall know her mind
In no man's love to bide.

Bind for her head a crown of crocuses,
And for her vest,
More fairy white than snow on upland wolds,
A posy of the flowers she loveth best,

CANZONE OF HYMNIA'S CORONATION

Stuck with marsh marigolds
And shy primroses and pale lady-smock,
Anemones that flock
In woody hollows where the dormice nest.
So in hedge-flowers and young crocuses
Let bosom and brows go drest.

FOR CECCO SLEEPY

Cecco's eyes begin to blink,
  Lay him down, lay him down !
Tired little head must sink,
  Little golden crown.

Cecco plays the valiant part
  All the day, all the day !
That's an eager little heart
  Tired out with play.

Sleep groweth masterful,
  Come to bed, come to bed !
Pillow deep in fleecy wool
  Cecco's nodding head.

50

FOR CECCO SLEEPY

Glozèd water, moon-dipt skies,
  Vague and deep, vague and deep!
That's the hue of Cecco's eyes
  Gossamer'd with sleep.

Eyelids flutter softly o'er,
  Snowy soft, snowy soft!
Kiss as lightly, sing no more;
  Folded is the croft.

Sigh of sea-breeze from the South,
  So, 'tis come! So, 'tis come!
Kiss his lids, from rosy mouth
  Draw a rosy thumb.

An some angel passing by
  Stoop to bless, stoop to bless!
Know, that little whisper'd sigh
  Is for happiness!

WHITE FLOWERS

White flowers, white flowers to deck my lady
    fair !
Clematis for her hair,
A cluster of vale lilies for her bosom
With apple blossom ;
Then out of open fields and grassy places
Pick her moon-daisies,
And make a wreath
With columbines and roses white as death :
Thus she will be
Smother'd in flower-foam, and live fragrantly.

Heap up a bank of white flowers for her feet ;
Bring meadow-sweet,
Bring her azaleas finer than spun silk,
Tuberose like frozen milk,

WHITE FLOWERS

And bloodless peonies, fresh-gather'd pinks;
Search on the brinks
Of rivers the great water-lily globe
Freed from its dark green robe:
Thus when my lady tireth she may tread
A bridal way to bed.

Bring flawless flowers,
And those that are more delicate than ours;
Love's votarist,
Shade her with lilies of the Eucharist
About her head;
Let myrtle and jasmine curtain up her bed,
Whose lingering scent
Shall lend her dreams perpetual ravishment:
Now, being kiss'd,
One crimson rose shall witness near her
        breast.

53

TO CROCUSES

I ASK you not, frail crocuses, that set
Light wings and thin
Alert to air still sharp with winter fret,
Bestow your innocence for coronet
Of me, stuck deep in sin ;
Yet suffer me to win
So much of outlook sober and demure
As yours, and pure,
That with your flush my spring-time may begin.

Whether upon the grass kirtled in white
(Snow drifted thither),
Or one by one, yet lingering and slight,
Your little fires broider a linkèd light,

TO CROCUSES

And beacon in black weather
The way for men, or whether,
More violet than heart of amethyst,
You kneel at rest
In folded peace, as nuns that pray together;

Let my upspringing be as glacial-clean,
And let me stand
Rejoicing in the sun-washt deep demesne
With you and all young flowers fresh and keen
As new rain on the land;
With you to lift up hand
Shrilling my orison at break of day,
Then bowing, say—
' We come and go, live, die, at God's command.'

Yours are mute raptures, silent ecstasies,
The secret song

SONGS

Of carven angel-brood whose litanies
Peal from wide-open eyes, and-like lilies
Are blown in a throng
By hidden wind and strong
About the fencèd garden, where the Maid
And Mother, having laid
To sleep her firstling, crooneth all day long.

O glad your coming, and your service glad,
Sweet-breathèd things ;
You look not to the prison once you had,
Take no thought wherewithal you shall be
    clad ;
You have no sorrowings,
Nor rankle of coward-stings ;
But speating ever upwards in your flight
You strain to light,
Then listen clear-eyed till the chant begins.

TO CROCUSES

If there is any music left in us,
Or any mirth
Whose song may well from hearts made
　　bounteous
As flows your still delight when, emulous,
Spring leaps from Winter's dearth,
Let such an equal worth
Of quiet-hued deliciousness be ours
That with your patient flowers
We fold on singing-robes to praise this
　　goodly earth.

SONG

Ask me not how much I love you;
Be content!
If too much love were sin
You would but win
Some of my punishment.
Ask me not, but believe I merely love you.

If indeed I truly love you,
Never more
Will any harm come near,
Nor need you fear
My heart's voice at the door
Of your heart, whisp'ring, Open, sweet,
  I love you.

SONG

See ! I cannot choose but love you
Soberly.
For, having felt your touch,
My pride in such
Familiarity
Warns me how he must worship who
    would love you.

SONG

O passion of the heart !
In whatso hidden chamber thou abidest,
Whereout on fire thou glidest
To film a glory round about our state ;
'Tis thy blood quickeneth
Our life that is thy death,
O heart most passionate !

Thine was that passioning heart
Of Italy, the blood
That fed her ; thine the art,
O Poet ! hers the flood
Of poisonous pride to spurn thee from her gate—
Thee ! that had crown'd her mistress of her fate.

SONG

O passion of the heart !
The burning heart of Dante, wing'd for serving,
Clove out a way unswerving
That led to deeper Hell, whence purified
It sought the Holy Place,
And lookt God in the face,
Then came back, sanctified.

High beat the stripling heart
That nine-year's day the Maid,
By Heaven throned apart,
Her great eyes unafraid
Lifted upon her guest, and that strong lover
Launcht his soul God's high secret to discover.

NESSUN MAGGIOR DOLORE

NEVER a sharper grief ·
Than remembrance of happy things
When our misery stings
And wounds ache for relief;

Never a wilder smart
Than love disclosed too late,
And the lover through the lockt gate
Showeth his bleeding heart;

Never more dolorous knell
Was sigh'd than Rimini's,
Francesca's the bride, and his
That loved too late and too well.

62

NESSUN MAGGIOR DOLORE

Never in all the hours
Of heart-breaking and keen
Pang of loss has there been
Love more fatal than ours !

DIRGE

How should my lord come home to his lands?
Alas for my lord, so brown and strong!
A lean cross in his folded hands,
And a daw to croak him a resting song.

And in autumn tide when the leaves fall down,
And wet falls as they fall, drip by drip,
My lord lies wan that once was so brown,
And the frost cometh to wither his lip.

My lord is white as the morning mist,
And his eyes ring'd like the winter moon:
And I will come as soon as ye list—
O love, is it time? May the time be soon!

64

FOR THE DEAD LORENZO

(FROM THE LATIN OF POLITIAN)

Who will grant to my head
Water?   Or who for mine eyes
Will open a fountain of tears ?
So that by night I may weep,
And may weep by day ;
Like as the dove widow'd is wont,
Or the swan that dieth is wont,
Like as the nightingale ;
Crying, Woe is for me !
Grief, ah, my grief !

SONGS

Our Tree [1] by the lightning shock
Lies cast suddenly down ;
Our Tree full of renown,
Famed where the Muses are
And famed where the wood-nymphs lie !
O Tree, whose clusterful boughs
Lent peace to the songs of Apollo,
And sweeten'd the sweet of his voice :—
Mute are the voices, alas !
And alas ! we are deaf that heard.

Who will grant to my head
Water ?   Or who for mine eyes
Will open a fountain of tears ?
So that by night I may weep,
And may weep by day ;
Like as the dove, widow'd, is wont,

---

[1] Of course Lorenzo, the *laurus*.

66

FOR THE DEAD LORENZO

Or the swan that dieth is wont,
Like as the nightingale :—
Crying, Woe is for me !
Grief, ah, my grief !

THE SPRING COPPICE

Ope your eyes, lift up your eyes,
Winds are blowing fair ;
Winds are fair and skies are true,
Frost shall never make you rue—
Spring is in the air ! .

Have no fear, what is to fear ?
Woods are washt and clean ;
Woods are dusted green and gold,
Gone are sourness, winter cold—
Loving-time is in.

Kiss their lids, the rosy lids
Vein'd and silver-rimm'd,

THE SPRING COPPICE

Blushes on them—kiss them, Wind,
Kiss and leave no sting behind
Lest the eyes be dimm'd.

White and gold, wood-flowers, behold !
Powder'd o'er the copse :
Woods yet faint, but ye are strong,
Lead the virginal prick-song
Till the music stops.

Wild hedge-buds, O dewy buds,
Laugh ye, strain and sing :
Sing till leaves your sun shall hide ;
Birds may hymn the Summer's pride—
Ye are gone with Spring.

Spring is shy, forward and shy,
Like a silly maid ;

SONGS

One that pouts when love is in,
Sighs that love may soon begin,
Droops her eyes and cocks her chin,
Eager and afraid.

Cuckoo call, O shout your call
Over wood and grass.
They will whisper it the river,
Life must leap or now or never—
Spring's a fickle lass !
Woo her then before she pass.

●

STORNELLI

Flower of the May !
What shall I do to make her forget me ?
She is so sad that should be so gay.

Ah, jessamine flower !
I toucht her hand and it set me on fire :
What would her lips do for power ?

O scarlet sorrel—
She that I love hath so pretty a rage
I love her wildest when she and I quarrel.

71

SONGS

Honey of lime !
Loving is easy ; but how to end loving !
Ah, that is harder than rhyme !

Wild purple heather,
You who have lain in her bosom this morn
Lie now in mine, and link us together.

ISEULT OF THE MILL

She stood among the budding grass,
The young man by her side.
He was so young,
She was so fair,
'Fore the Mass, they made a lovely pair
All the yellow eventide,
With O the swathes of grass!

When the moon rose it came to pass
The maid sat there alone.
One hand on her chin,
One hand to her side,
Where her heart throbb'd the wound did
    chide:

SONGS

The grieving bird with her made moan,
With, Woe's my love, alas!

"Kissing her is but to be stung:
"Ware shrew!" said the swain.
"She is too fell,
"I am too meek."
She had an angry spot in each cheek,
She drove him out with her disdain:
Sing, Woe! the scolding tongue.

ARIADNE FORSAKEN

(CHORUS FROM A PLAY)

I

HE swept remorse from his eyes; with un-
  staying feet
For the foam-bitten shores
He hasten'd, hounded by Fate.
Soon shall the sails, like cliffs, cover the fleet,
The sea flash white to the freight,
The pulse and the thresh of the oars.
Wingèd man, born of woman, outsoars
The hawk in his flight: he falleth anon and
  outpours
His eager estate.

SONGS

II

The Olympian breathed with his mouth, the hero
    passionate-blind,
Drave where he led
As a ship whose helmsman is gone;
Yea, as a ship smitten, curst by the wind,
He went out muttering, wan;
He spake not, turn'd not his head.
Where is the chaplet of love?   It is faded, is
    dead!
Woe to the Spousal, the Bride, the desolate bed,
Loveless, alone!

III

Woman that liveth to love, to trust, and to cling,
Being forsworn,

Choketh the tears as they start,

Masketh the glint of her passion, traileth her
wing

As a bird, grieveth apart,

Tearless, voiceless, forlorn.

Ripple of laughing and speech hath she to love ;
but to mourn,

Tempest of sighs, and labouring bosom, and
shorn

Hair, and dead heart.

IV

Man that is born of woman, purposeful, bound,

Lifteth his eyes

To the wild splendour of God,

Dazed and blinded : Earth he loveth, her sound

As of flutes and reed-music, her load

Of beauty and ecstasies.

But how shall he know to love the terrors, the
  mysteries,
The hush of the silence, the brooding, the still
  surprise,
The awful Abode?

v

This is the lot of a woman, she boweth her
  knees,
Yieldeth her limbs,
Giveth her candour, her untrodden soul,
Into thy keeping, O man ! For lordship she sees
Thron'd on thy brows, and control.
Lit by thy favour she swims
Halo'd about with the sun of thy smiling, and
  hymns
Hymeneal, with odours of myrtle, and dreams
Golden and whole !

VI

Whenas the bruit of the battle, and lust of the
    war,
The smell of the sea,
Drive thee abroad, she cannot gainsay
Aught of thy purpose, O man; but dumbly afar
Setteth her eyes to the day:
She bendeth her knee.
Hope against hope! for the strength of the God
    is on thee,
Fever of blood-thirst, passion that tangles the
    free,
Have thee for prey.

VII

Power have Gods to drive us whither they will,
Humble our knees,
Lure us to ruin and sin:

Power to whelm, spurn, madden, and kill;

Crave us they may, net, and fasten us in,

Launch us on desolate seas!

Such might have the Gods, and power; but no peace

Follows them there.   Men they may bind at their ease,

But their love never win!

MEDITATIONS

F

FLOS VIRGINUM

Where is a holier thing
In a fair world apparell'd for our bliss
Than the pure influence
That dwells in a girl's heart
And beams from her quiet eyes?
Earth has no ministering
So lovely, so acceptable or wise,
Withal so frail as this;
Which, if man win, it needeth all his art,
Lest uncouth violence,
Rough mastery, or the tyrannies of earth,
Should maim or shatter out
With ill-timed speech or flout
Her wistful-tender'd balm at very birth.

MEDITATIONS

Her Motherhood to be
She hides in her child-bosom, as a seed
That creepeth to be flower
Long ere it feeleth light :
She nurtureth her lover.
Within her arms made free,
Upon her heart made restful, given over
To her most gentle deed,
He lieth watcht upon by her grave sight ;
And she liveth her hour,
Contented to be Mother to this child,
Given before her time
Assurance whence to climb
Up to her real throne of Godhead mild.

Then in her perfect day,
Whenas her sanguine flower hath burst
    the sheath,

FLOS VIRGINUM

And she, a maiden tall,
Doth soberly give up
Her sanctity and grace,
Her childhood's free array,
To win her order'd and appointed place ;
Submissness as a wreath
Lieth upon her; and she is a cup
Of bounties unto all.
So all that come about her worship her,
And in her pleasance find
Peace and a quiet mind,
Her pledge of honour, and her harbinger.

When the crown of her flesh,
New flesh ensoul'd from her saint armoury
Of pure flesh sublimated,
Is set upon her brows,
All her strength she will give

MEDITATIONS

To draw it out from the mesh
Of circumstance adverse, that so it live
And grow to bud, as she
Herself from grafted slip became a rose ;
Her prayer is consummated
In her meek mercies and her tenderness
For this groping and blind
Whisper of love behind,
And stronger cry of joy and thankfulness.

Ah, frailer than a breath,
Sullied sooner, more fatally than glass !
If such most desolate
Pitiful lot be hers,
That a brute-soul possess
And goad her to her death ;
Death were more welcome than the piteousness
Of life, for she would pass

FLOS VIRGINUM

Up to the stars, the silent messengers
Of God who from his seat
Weepeth for beauty driven down by dearth
Of love to peak and fail,
To wring hands and turn pale,
Eyeing dismay'd the shock of her soul's worth.

PREPARATION

I ARISE to anoint my soul
With the unction of her sweet breath,
To bathe and wash in the light
Of her eyes clearer than snow.
Her eyes are like hyacinth,
And deep as the sea, and dark
As the hold of the mountain water.
To-day, in an hour, she and I
Will be face to face : from her eyes
Her startled soul will look out,
And mine will be comforted
To lend comfort to hers.

PREPARATION

Ah, Saint Lucy, whose light
Ceased not with breath, nor was quencht
Under the knife-edge !   Now
With the scars heal'd you are come,
Stoopt from heaven to earth :
And your eyes kindle and burn,
Gleam insurgent, are dewy
Like April blotted in tears,
Or quick to the Sun.   Laugh now !
Laugh now, let no crying
Beat at your heart's shut door
For the treasure hidden and held.

Ah, little Maid !
Ah, little Queen, crown'd and raised up above,
Are you afraid ?
Are you tremulous, fearing the accolade
Of my singing of love ?

MEDITATIONS

The flutter'd heart of a bird
Throbs thro' his wing ; your heart
Cries in your mutinous mouth,
In your wide eyes, in your meek
Hands folded and still !
Give me your two hands—so ; let me hold
    and kneel
Till the tempest be done,
And the sun shine over your face.

'DONNA È GENTIL—'

Thy lonely virginal air,
And thy vague eyes,
The carven stillness of thy sorrowful
    mouth,
And sanctity of thy youth,
Mark thee for no man's prize:
Set thee apart to be fair,
Holy, lovely, and wise.

Being so fair thou art holy
Even as Beatrice is:
Sister-torches of God,
Twin pastures untrod,
Handmaidens meek and lowly,

MEDITATIONS

Consecrate priestesses,
To Heaven dedicate wholly.

Thy face drinketh the light!
Moon-lit, girdled with stars,
Sapphire-gemm'd and adorn'd,
Thou art that lamp which burn'd
From the beginning! The bars
Of Wisdom were overturn'd:
Innocence claim'd her birthright.

In the clear spaces of Heaven
As sisters and lovers sit
Beatrice and Thou embraced,
Hand and hand, waist and waist,
And smile at the worship given
By Earth, and the men in it
To whom you were manifest.

'DONNA È GENTIL—'

And because I have loved you well,
And because I was born for this
(As the great Tuscan was born
To love and serve Beatrice),
I, who have suffer'd all scorn,
Spend my treasure to tell
All your high worthiness.

ROSA NASCOSA

MORE than those
Enfranchised beauties her perfection shows,
Like a concealèd rose,
But to the thickets where she lieth close.

These libertines
Encompass her with hardy-visaged spines ;
She frets not nor repines,
But does their bidding meekly, and resigns

Herself to be
Their bond-servant, who should be more
    than free ;
Having a liberty
There where her soul can fear no enemy.

ROSA NASCOSA

There she doth find,
All broad dominion and a heaven all kind,
In her unravisht mind
Whereto her brute possessioners are blind.

Possession goes
No deeper than the surface ; there are mines
Far down, whose sacred fee
And golden hold no trammelling can bind.

ARTEMISION

Now Winter stealeth out like a white nun,
  Cloaking her face behind her icy fingers,
And men each day look longer at the Sun,
  While late and later yet the sweet light
    lingers.

Fast by the hedgerows, bit by gales of March,
  A chaplet for thy brows of delicate leaves—
Tendrils of briony, ruby tufts of larch,
  Woodsorrel, crocus pale, the New Year weaves.

Yet is thy smile half wintry, as forlorn
  To view thy state too solemn for thy years,

ARTEMISION

And half amazèd as a flower's, late born,
    And not more quick for pleasure than for
    tears.

Thy month austere telleth thy cloistral fashion :
March frost thy pride is, March wind thy pent
    passion.

SAINT BEAUTY

'Or pensa quanta bellezza avea . . . che nessuno che la vedesse mai la guardò per concupiscenza, tanto era la santità che rilustrava in lei.'—SAVONAROLA.

IN chamber thought my mind is like a fire
   Kindled and set to roar by a strong wind,
   And my tongue eloquent, and my eyes blind
To all but mad pursuit of their desire.
But I am mute before thee, as a quire
   Of singers when one chant soars unconfin'd
   From one gold-throated minstrel : thou dost
      bind
My lips, eyes, heart, my very thought's attire.
   For body's beauty is thy soul's thin veil

SAINT BEAUTY

Wherethro' soul's beauty shineth like a jewel
  Blood-bright, whose too pure strength would
      else assail
    Earth-groping eyes : it hath thy soul's im-
      press,
It hath thy soul's white magic, but, less cruel,
  Soul's pride softened by body's courteous-
      ness.

EROS NARCISSUS

If I should force the sentries of her lips,
    What should it profit me, to shock her soul?
Or see young Faith in pitiful eclipse,
    Or watch her don Abasement's leaden stole?

If I should bid her tell me all her love,
    Bare all the rosy secret of her heart;
What gain, to see her spoil herself thereof?
    For her what gain, to see her love depart?

Her lovely mystery is her loveliness,
    And her sweet reticence her seal of price;

EROS-NARCISSUS

For what she loveth darkly that she is—
Priestess, communicant, and sacrifice.

In her own mould she fashions Love, and he
Scarce knows himself, vested so tenderly.

THAT STONE WALLS CAN NEVER SEPARATE
HIM FROM HIS LADY

NEVER the shadow of a summer cloud
   Can fleet between my Lady and my loving;
The miser World shall find my head unbow'd
   And my heart's temper high beyond its proving.

My heart is fixt to be her Prisoner,
   And she, an honest Janitress, the keys
Doth shrine in her own heart as Treasurer,
   So sure that Death itself were not Decease.

For if upon a day Fate proved unkind
   And grimly stalkt betwixt my Love and me,

THE INSEPARABLE LOVER

The glancing motions of her faithful mind
   Would glint athwart him plain for me to see:

And in her beamy light above his shroud
I'd see her smile, gay, confident, and proud.

HIS LADY A THIEF

THAT intercourse with thee I have in dreams
    But serves to whet my anguish to be reft,
Not of thy sight which visits me in gleams,
    But of my consciousness of thy sweet theft.

Thou wert the thief of me, and I, the thiev'd,
    Felt such great riches viewing thee in act
To rob me daily, nothing less I griev'd
    Than being accessory to thy fact.

Now by a forced decree love to the lover
    Is render'd back, it hath no further use

HIS LADY A THIEF

Than stare reproach at him who gave it over,
  And lookt to gain by so much he did lose.

O my blest thief, come rifle all my treasure;
I cannot love but only out of measure!

HAVING LOST HIS LADY

Had I but loved her as I ought
  Instead of as she would,
Following the tenour of my thought
  And heedless of her mood,

Inaction had obtain'd what now
  By shock of arms is lost;
Beleaguer'd ladies soonest bow
  Their heads, like flowers, to frost.

But or too courteous was I
  Indifference to feign,
Or too solicitous to buy
  Ease from my private pain.

106

HAVING LOST HIS LADY

Like one who, burning, seeks new fire
   From that which made him smart,
Or o'er desirous begs desire
   Ere he hath rid his heart;

Surfeited frenzy I did win,
   And woke not love but dread:
There shall no traveller to that inn
   Where clamour makes the bed.

PROMETHEUS

THAT most fatally dower'd,
Prometheus, of all men's seed,
Lifted up restless eyes
From our most gentle earth,
And sought the glint of the skies,
And stole immortal fire
To our immortal woe.

For that keen flame of Heaven,
Swifter than glancing light
Or leap of sound, than the air
More subtle, than day more bright—
Thought, which to God is given
Creative, is our despair,
And a load we cannot bear.

PROMETHEUS

It burneth in the brain,
It throbbeth deep in the heart,
Before its blade our eyes
Dazzle, we reel and go
Whither our hot thought flies,
Up to the deathless Gods,
Then cry, In vain !   It is vain !

Man is a cage of pain,
His thought is a pure thin fire
That beateth against the bars
And bonds of his grosser part,
Astrain for the sky.   And behold
The flame roareth and rendeth,
And the war nor stayeth nor endeth !

Then at last when the bars
Of the body shatter'd and torn

MEDITATIONS

Cleave asunder, the flame
Winneth the bitter stars
(Keener than scimitars),
And man lieth prone in shame :
Better not to be born !

SONG AND ART

Art, the delicate boy,
And Song, his little half-brother,
Both were children of Love ;
But Song had Tears for his Mother,
And Art was issue of Joy.

Song shed on us like rain
The stream of his murmur'd story,
And Art was our masterful sun
When the morning utter'd his glory,
And the flowers drank and were fain.

III

MEDITATIONS

Song pluckt the strings of the heart ;
Crying and high possession
Held the soul as he sway'd :
The pride of the eyes and the passion
Of the stirr'd sense held Art.

Grief and the grace of speech
Song gave men from his Mother ;
And Art gave laughing and joy.
But brother coveted brother
His birthright, and each grudged each.

Art had commerce with Pain ;
She bit him and led him a-sinning ;
And Song threw over his harp,
For he saw a Corybant grinning,
And piped to her mad refrain.

SONG AND ART

Art, the delicate boy,
And Song, his little half-brother,
Both the children of Love—
Song in blood drown'd his Mother,
And Art grew to stifle Joy.

SHAKESPEARE IN CHURCH

In the grey church, by the slow river side,
  Hard by the altar, calling the altar's God,
  That one who erst had spread his wings abroad
And sail'd remote in dim great worlds and wide,
Knowing the mystery of them, and the pride
  Of kingship over them that earth-ways trod,
  Prouder than Pride and greater, kist the rod,
Took up the Cross, and, calling on Christ, died.
His grave long vision that swept beyond our ken
  Saw golden Harmony, steadfast passionless
    Measure,
  And Order stablisht by divine decree ;

Knew those who bent to Destiny, bravest men,
    That with unwinking eyes did God's good
        pleasure :
    He therefore, soul upright, did bend his
        knee.

GULLS ON THE THAMES

From what long shore, O wastrel company!
  Come on the pulse of what distressful wings?
What discord internecine sunders ye
  Each from his fellow, stony-hearted kings
O' the air, sailing remote, askance?   The sea
  Storm-tost and black reckt not your hanker-
      ings,
But drove you like a snow-cloud from her lee,
  To bicker and swoop o'er sodden river things.
Like snowflakes in a riot of unrest
  They drift athwart the winter beam o' the sun,

GULLS ON THE THAMES

Wrangling and battling their wild wings,
    and scream
Harsh challenge; or deep-nested in the
    stream
Search the waste waters desolate and dun;
Then beating upwards urge their clamorous
    quest.

BALLAD OF CLYTIÉ

HEARKEN, O passers, what thing
Fortuned in Hellas.   A maid,
Lissom and white as the roe,
Lived recess'd in a glade.
Clytié, Hamadryad,
She was called that I sing—
Flower so fair, so frail, that to bring her
    a woe,
Surely a pitiful thing !

A wild bright creature of trees,
Brooks, and the sun among leaves,
Clytié, grown to be maid :
Ah, she had eyes like the sea's

BALLAD OF CLYTIÉ

Iris of green and blue !
White as sea-foam her brows,
And her hair reedy and gold :
So she grew and waxt supple and fit to be
    spouse
In a king's palace of old.

All in a kirtle of green,
With her tangle of red-gold hair,
In the live heart of an oak,
Clytié, harbouring there,
Thronèd there as a queen,
Clytié wondering woke :
Ah, child, what set thee too high for thy
    sweet demesne,
And who ponder'd the doleful stroke ?

For the child that was maiden grown,
The queen of the forest places,

MEDITATIONS

Clytié, Hamadryad,
Tired of the joy she had,
And the kingdom that was her own ;
And tired of the quick wood-races,
And joy of herself in the pool when she
    wonder'd down,
And tired of her budded graces.

And the child lookt up to the Sun
And the burning track of his car
In the broad serene above her :
' O King Sun, be thou my lover,
For my beauty is just begun.
I am fresh and fair as a star ;
Come, lie where the lilies are :
Behold, I am fair and dainty and white
    all over,
And I waste in the wood unknown ! '

BALLAD OF CLYTIÉ

Rose-flusht, daring, she strain'd
Her young arms up, and she voiced
The wild desire of her heart.
The woodland heard her, the faun,
The satyr, and things that start,
Peering, heard her; the dove, crooning,
    complain'd
In the pine-tree hard by the lawn.
Only the runnel rejoiced
In his rushy hollow apart
To see her beauty flash up
White and red as the dawn.

Sorrow, ye passers-by,
The quick lift of her word,
The crimson blush of her pride !
Heard her the heavens' lord
In his flaming seat in the sky:

MEDITATIONS

'Overbold of her years that will not be denied;
She would be the Sun-God's bride!'
His brow it was like the flat of a sword,
And levin the glance of his side.

For he bent unto her, and his mouth
Burnt her like coals of fire;
He gazed with passionate eyes,
Like flame that kindles and dries,
And his breath suckt hers as the white rage
    of the South
Draws life; his desire
Was like to a tiger's drouth.
What shall the slim maiden avail?
Alas, and alas for her youth!

Tremble, O maids, that would set
Your love-longing to the Sun!

BALLAD OF CLYTIÉ

For Clytié mourn, and take heed
How she loved her king and did bleed
Ere kissing had yet begun.
For lo! one shaft from his terrible eyes she
    met,
And it burnt to her soul, and anon
She paled, and the fever-fret
Did bite to her bones; and wan
She fell to rueing the deed.

Mark ye, maidens, and cower!
Lo, for an end of breath,
Clytié, hardy and frail,
Anguisht after her death.
For the Sun-flower droops and is pale
When her king hideth his power,
And ever draggeth the woe of her piteous
    tale,

MEDITATIONS

As a woman that laboureth
Yet never reacheth the hour :
So Clytié yearns to the Sun, for her wraith
Moans in the bow'd sun-flower.

Clytié, Hamadryad,
Called was she that I sing :
Flower so fair and frail that to work her
    this woe,
Surely a pitiful thing !

LA PIA

' *Siena mi fè*, *disfecemi Maremma.*'

THE dark is round me like a bed ;
I push the hair from off my face :
That blue line, like a little thread
Is all the hint in this deep place
That the sun still shines overhead.

I wait the moment it begins,
From where I crouch on hands and knees
I watch it as it fills and thins
And think I hear the wistful trees :
It seemeth summer till it dims.

125

MEDITATIONS

Siena was the stony hold
Where I was cradled.   Ere my years
Twice seven winter times had told
Set in a moon that froze my tears,
And I, that knew not youth, was old.

He ringed me on the wedding hand,
For thus were maidens bought and sold,
And dower'd me with house and land,
And kist me : but my lips were cold,
My knees shook that I scarce could stand.

My fief was all that windy house
Whose entry lock was like a fang ;
Alone I was with bat and mouse
Whenas the door had ceased its clang,
And him that was the lord of us.

LA PIA

Sometimes he call'd me 'little child,'
And set his long hand to my hair;
And he would laugh when I lookt wild,
To eye him like a crippled hare.
I feared him chiefest when he smiled.

His smile was like a starven man's
That waits until his friend shall die,
And laughs as madmen laugh, and plans
His glut of hatred by-and-by,
And feeds his hunger as he scans.

Still in my vigils I can view
Maremma glimmer like a sea
Towards that other sea whose hue
And limit touch eternity,
And touching melt blue into blue.

127

MEDITATIONS

He was beside me those long days,
His terror made me cold o' nights :
He scarcely spoke or fixèd gaze
Upon me, yet the shifty lights
Of his chill eyes followed my ways.

Once he did laugh on me, then frown'd
Because I ran and clutcht the door;
Once more he laught that day he found
My eyes grown hollow : yet once more—
'Tis that which haunts me underground.

I am too thin to rise and wail,
I am too chill to be athirst;
I cannot pray, I am too frail
To shriek my sorrow if I durst:
No one can see how I am pale.

LA PIA

I have not grace enough to die;
I have no friend; there is no God.
I bit my lip till it ran dry
To write my legend in my blood
On the bare wall 'gainst which I lie.

That on the day when I am dead—
For to all men cometh to die
At last—who leaneth o'er my bed
With a struck light to see me by,
May know this dark made me afraid.

THE SAINTS' MAYING

Since green earth is awake
Let us now pastime take,
Not serving wantonness
Too well, nor niggardess,
Which monks of men would make.

But clothed like earth in green,
With jocund hearts and clean,
We will take hands and go
Singing where quietly blow
The flowers of Spring's demesne.

130

THE SAINTS' MAYING

The cuckoo haileth loud
The open sky; no cloud
Doth fleck the earth's blue tent;
The land laughs, well content
To put off winter shroud.

Now, since 'tis Easter Day,
All Christians may have play;
The young Saints, all agaze
For Christ in Heaven's maze,
May laugh who wont to pray.

Then welcome to our round
They light on homely ground :—
Agnes, Saint Cecily,
Agatha, Dorothy,
Margaret, Hildegonde;

MEDITATIONS

Next come with Barbara
Lucy and Ursula ;
And last, queen of the Nine,
Clear-eyed Saint Catherine
Joyful arrayeth her.

Then chooseth each her lad,
And after frolic had
Of dance and carolling
And playing in a ring,
Seek all the woodland shade.

And there for each his lass
Her man a nosegay has,
Which better than word spoken
Might stand to be her token
And emblem of her grace.

132

THE SAINTS' MAYING

For Cecily, who bent
Her slim white neck and went
To Heaven a virgin still,
The nodding daffodil
That bends but is not shent.

Lucy, whose wounded eyes
Opened in Heaven star-wise,
The lady-smock, whose light
Doth prank the grass with white,
Taketh for badge and prize.

Because for Lord Christ's hest
Men shore thy warm bright breast,
Agatha, see thy part
Showed in the burning heart
Of the white crocus best.

MEDITATIONS

What fate was Barbara's
Shut in the tower of brass,
We figure and hold up
Within the stiff king-cup
That crowns the meadow grass.

Agnes, than whose King Death
Stayed no more delicate breath
On earth, we give for dower
Wood-sorrel, that frail flower
That Spring first quickeneth.

Dorothy, whose shrill voice
Bade Heathendom rejoice,
The sweet-breath'd cowslip hath ;
And Margaret, who in death
Saw Heaven, her pearly choice.

134

THE SAINTS' MAYING

Then she of virgin brood
Whom Prince of Britain woo'd,
Ursula, takes by favour
The hyacinth whose savour
Enskies the sunny wood.

Hildegonde, whose spirit high
The Cross did not deny,
Yet blusht to feel the shame,
Anemones must claim,
Whose roses early die.

Last, she who gave in pledge
Her neck to the wheel's edge,
Taketh the fresh primrose
Which (even as she her foes)
Redeems the wintry hedge.

MEDITATIONS

So garlanded, entwined,
Each as may prompt her mind,
The Saints renew for Earth
And Heaven such seemly mirth
As God once had design'd.

And when the day is done,
And veil'd the goodly Sun,
Each man his maid by right
Doth kiss and bid Good-night;
And home goes every one.

The maids to Heaven do hie
To serve God soberly;
The lads, their loves in Heaven,
What lowly work is given
They do to win the sky.

THE END